Healthy Desserts: 50 Guilt-Free Recipes

By: Kelly Johnson

Table of Contents

- Avocado Chocolate Mousse
- Banana Oatmeal Cookies
- Almond Butter Chocolate Cups
- Chia Seed Pudding
- Coconut Macaroons
- Greek Yogurt Parfait with Berries
- Baked Apple with Cinnamon
- Chocolate-Covered Strawberries
- Almond Flour Brownies
- Coconut Flour Cupcakes
- Banana Ice Cream
- Chia Chocolate Energy Bites
- Sugar-Free Lemon Bars
- Pumpkin Spice Protein Balls
- Coconut Milk Rice Pudding
- Apple Cinnamon Baked Donuts
- Carrot Cake Energy Bites
- Chocolate Banana Bread
- Blueberry Almond Crumble
- Lemon Coconut Bliss Balls
- Sweet Potato Brownies
- Raw Vegan Cheesecake
- Dark Chocolate Almond Bark
- Strawberry Chia Jam
- Baked Peaches with Greek Yogurt
- Oatmeal Raisin Cookies
- Chocolate Avocado Truffles
- Raw Energy Bars
- Date and Nut Energy Balls
- Matcha Protein Balls
- Peach Sorbet
- Mocha Protein Ice Cream
- Zucchini Chocolate Cake
- Almond Joy Protein Bars
- Chocolate-Covered Almonds

- Sweet Potato Pie Smoothie
- Chia Coconut Bars
- Baked Coconut Donuts
- Vegan Chocolate Chip Cookies
- Coconut Lime Popsicles
- Healthy Fruit Tarts
- Raspberry Almond Muffins
- Chocolate Peanut Butter Energy Bites
- Coconut Yogurt Parfaits
- Dark Chocolate Coconut Energy Bites
- Pina Colada Protein Smoothie
- Raspberry Sorbet
- Avocado Lime Cheesecake
- Coconut Pudding Cups
- Apple Crisp with Oat Topping

Avocado Chocolate Mousse

Ingredients

- 2 ripe avocados, peeled and pitted
- 1/4 cup cocoa powder
- 1/4 cup maple syrup or honey
- 1 teaspoon vanilla extract
- Pinch of salt
- 2-3 tablespoons almond milk or any milk of your choice

Instructions

1. In a food processor or blender, combine the avocado, cocoa powder, maple syrup, vanilla extract, and salt.
2. Blend until smooth, scraping down the sides as needed.
3. Add almond milk, one tablespoon at a time, until you reach your desired consistency.
4. Spoon into serving dishes and chill for at least 30 minutes before serving.
5. Serve as is, or top with fresh berries or a sprinkle of shaved chocolate.

Banana Oatmeal Cookies

Ingredients

- 2 ripe bananas, mashed
- 1 1/2 cups rolled oats
- 1/4 cup almond butter or peanut butter
- 1/4 cup dark chocolate chips (optional)
- 1 teaspoon vanilla extract
- 1/2 teaspoon cinnamon
- Pinch of salt

Instructions

1. Preheat the oven to 350°F (175°C).
2. In a bowl, mix the mashed bananas, oats, almond butter, vanilla extract, cinnamon, and salt until combined.
3. Stir in the chocolate chips, if using.
4. Drop spoonfuls of the dough onto a baking sheet lined with parchment paper.
5. Bake for 10-12 minutes, or until golden brown on the edges.
6. Let cool before serving.

Almond Butter Chocolate Cups

Ingredients

- 1 cup almond butter
- 1/4 cup honey or maple syrup
- 1 teaspoon vanilla extract
- 1 cup dark chocolate chips
- Pinch of salt

Instructions

1. Line a muffin tin with paper cupcake liners.
2. In a bowl, mix together the almond butter, honey, vanilla extract, and a pinch of salt.
3. Spoon a small amount of the almond butter mixture into the bottom of each muffin liner.
4. In a microwave-safe bowl, melt the dark chocolate chips in 30-second intervals, stirring after each interval.
5. Spoon the melted chocolate over the almond butter mixture in the muffin liners.
6. Place the tin in the freezer for 1-2 hours until the cups are firm.
7. Remove from the tin and store in the refrigerator.

Chia Seed Pudding

Ingredients

- 1/4 cup chia seeds
- 1 cup almond milk (or any milk of choice)
- 1 tablespoon maple syrup or honey
- 1/2 teaspoon vanilla extract
- Fresh fruit or nuts for topping

Instructions

1. In a bowl, whisk together the chia seeds, almond milk, maple syrup, and vanilla extract.
2. Cover and refrigerate for at least 4 hours or overnight, allowing the chia seeds to absorb the liquid and thicken.
3. Stir well before serving.
4. Top with fresh fruit, nuts, or granola of your choice.

Coconut Macaroons

Ingredients

- 2 1/2 cups unsweetened shredded coconut
- 2/3 cup egg whites (about 4 large eggs)
- 1/3 cup honey or maple syrup
- 1 teaspoon vanilla extract
- Pinch of salt

Instructions

1. Preheat the oven to 325°F (165°C).
2. In a large bowl, mix together the shredded coconut, egg whites, honey, vanilla extract, and salt.
3. Drop spoonfuls of the mixture onto a baking sheet lined with parchment paper.
4. Bake for 15-20 minutes, or until golden brown on top.
5. Let cool before serving.

Greek Yogurt Parfait with Berries

Ingredients

- 2 cups Greek yogurt
- 1 tablespoon honey or maple syrup
- 1 cup mixed berries (strawberries, blueberries, raspberries)
- 1/4 cup granola

Instructions

1. In a bowl, mix the Greek yogurt with honey or maple syrup.
2. Layer the yogurt in serving glasses or bowls, alternating with layers of mixed berries and granola.
3. Top with more berries and a drizzle of honey.
4. Serve immediately or refrigerate for a few hours for a chilled treat.

Baked Apple with Cinnamon

Ingredients

- 4 apples, cored
- 1/4 cup raisins
- 1 tablespoon cinnamon
- 1 tablespoon honey or maple syrup
- 1/4 cup water

Instructions

1. Preheat the oven to 350°F (175°C).
2. Place the cored apples in a baking dish.
3. Stuff the center of each apple with raisins and sprinkle with cinnamon.
4. Drizzle honey or maple syrup over the apples and add water to the bottom of the baking dish.
5. Cover with foil and bake for 30-40 minutes, or until the apples are tender.
6. Serve warm as a cozy dessert.

Chocolate-Covered Strawberries

Ingredients

- 12 large strawberries, washed and dried
- 4 oz dark chocolate or milk chocolate, chopped
- 1 tablespoon coconut oil (optional)

Instructions

1. Melt the chocolate and coconut oil (if using) in a heatproof bowl over a double boiler or in the microwave in 30-second intervals.
2. Dip each strawberry into the melted chocolate, coating it halfway.
3. Place the dipped strawberries on a parchment-lined tray and let the chocolate harden in the fridge for about 30 minutes.
4. Serve chilled as a sweet treat.

Almond Flour Brownies

Ingredients

- 2 cups almond flour
- 1/2 cup unsweetened cocoa powder
- 1/4 cup maple syrup or honey
- 3 large eggs
- 1/4 cup coconut oil, melted
- 1 teaspoon vanilla extract
- 1/4 teaspoon baking soda
- Pinch of salt

Instructions

1. Preheat the oven to 350°F (175°C).
2. In a large bowl, whisk together the almond flour, cocoa powder, baking soda, and salt.
3. In another bowl, whisk the eggs, maple syrup, melted coconut oil, and vanilla extract.
4. Combine the wet and dry ingredients and mix until smooth.
5. Pour the batter into a greased 8x8-inch baking pan.
6. Bake for 20-25 minutes, or until a toothpick inserted in the center comes out clean.
7. Let cool before slicing and serving.

Coconut Flour Cupcakes

Ingredients

- 1/2 cup coconut flour
- 1/4 cup almond flour
- 1/4 cup honey or maple syrup
- 4 large eggs
- 1/4 cup coconut oil, melted
- 1 teaspoon vanilla extract
- 1/2 teaspoon baking powder
- Pinch of salt

Instructions

1. Preheat the oven to 350°F (175°C) and line a muffin tin with paper liners.
2. In a bowl, whisk together the coconut flour, almond flour, baking powder, and salt.
3. In a separate bowl, beat the eggs, honey, coconut oil, and vanilla extract until smooth.
4. Gradually combine the dry ingredients with the wet ingredients, mixing until well combined.
5. Spoon the batter into the muffin tin, filling each cup about 2/3 full.
6. Bake for 18-22 minutes, or until a toothpick inserted comes out clean.
7. Let the cupcakes cool before serving.

Banana Ice Cream

Ingredients

- 3 ripe bananas, sliced and frozen
- 1 teaspoon vanilla extract
- 1/4 cup almond milk (optional)
- Toppings (chocolate chips, nuts, berries, etc.)

Instructions

1. Place the frozen banana slices into a food processor or high-speed blender.
2. Blend until smooth and creamy, scraping down the sides as needed.
3. If the mixture is too thick, add almond milk a tablespoon at a time until the desired consistency is reached.
4. Add vanilla extract and blend again.
5. Serve immediately as soft-serve, or transfer to a container and freeze for an hour for a firmer texture.
6. Top with your favorite toppings and enjoy!

Chia Chocolate Energy Bites

Ingredients

- 1 cup rolled oats
- 1/4 cup chia seeds
- 1/4 cup cacao powder
- 1/4 cup almond butter
- 1/4 cup honey or maple syrup
- 1/4 cup dark chocolate chips (optional)
- 1 teaspoon vanilla extract

Instructions

1. In a bowl, mix together the oats, chia seeds, and cacao powder.
2. Add the almond butter, honey, and vanilla extract. Stir until well combined.
3. If desired, add chocolate chips and mix again.
4. Roll the mixture into small balls, about 1-inch in diameter.
5. Place the energy bites on a parchment-lined tray and refrigerate for at least 30 minutes.
6. Store in an airtight container in the fridge for up to a week.

Sugar-Free Lemon Bars

Ingredients

- 1 1/2 cups almond flour
- 1/4 cup coconut flour
- 1/4 teaspoon baking powder
- 1/2 cup butter, softened
- 1/4 cup erythritol or your preferred sugar substitute
- 3 large eggs
- 1/2 cup fresh lemon juice
- 1 tablespoon lemon zest
- 1/4 teaspoon salt

Instructions

1. Preheat the oven to 350°F (175°C) and line an 8x8-inch baking dish with parchment paper.
2. In a bowl, mix almond flour, coconut flour, baking powder, and salt.
3. In another bowl, beat together the butter and erythritol until creamy.
4. Add the eggs, one at a time, followed by the lemon juice and zest.
5. Gradually add the dry ingredients to the wet mixture, stirring until smooth.
6. Pour the batter into the prepared dish and bake for 20-25 minutes, or until set and slightly golden.
7. Let cool before cutting into squares.

Pumpkin Spice Protein Balls

Ingredients

- 1/2 cup pumpkin puree
- 1/2 cup rolled oats
- 1/4 cup vanilla protein powder
- 1/4 cup almond butter
- 1 teaspoon pumpkin spice
- 1 tablespoon honey
- 1/4 teaspoon cinnamon
- Pinch of salt

Instructions

1. In a bowl, mix together the pumpkin puree, oats, protein powder, almond butter, pumpkin spice, cinnamon, honey, and salt.
2. Stir until the mixture is well combined.
3. Roll the mixture into small balls, about 1 inch in diameter.
4. Place the balls on a tray and refrigerate for at least 30 minutes before serving.
5. Store in an airtight container in the fridge for up to a week.

Coconut Milk Rice Pudding

Ingredients

- 1 cup Arborio rice
- 2 1/2 cups coconut milk
- 1/4 cup honey or maple syrup
- 1 teaspoon vanilla extract
- 1/2 teaspoon cinnamon
- Pinch of salt

Instructions

1. In a medium saucepan, combine the rice, coconut milk, honey, vanilla, cinnamon, and salt.
2. Bring to a boil, then reduce heat to low.
3. Simmer, stirring occasionally, for 25-30 minutes, or until the rice is tender and the pudding has thickened.
4. Remove from heat and let cool for a few minutes.
5. Serve warm or chilled, topped with additional cinnamon or fruit if desired.

Apple Cinnamon Baked Donuts

Ingredients

- 1 cup almond flour
- 1/2 cup coconut flour
- 1/2 teaspoon baking soda
- 1 teaspoon cinnamon
- 2 large eggs
- 1/4 cup unsweetened applesauce
- 2 tablespoons honey or maple syrup
- 1 teaspoon vanilla extract
- 1/4 teaspoon salt

Instructions

1. Preheat the oven to 350°F (175°C) and grease a donut pan.
2. In a bowl, combine almond flour, coconut flour, baking soda, cinnamon, and salt.
3. In another bowl, whisk together the eggs, applesauce, honey, and vanilla extract.
4. Gradually add the dry ingredients to the wet ingredients, mixing until smooth.
5. Spoon the batter into the donut pan, filling each mold about 3/4 full.
6. Bake for 12-15 minutes, or until a toothpick inserted comes out clean.
7. Let cool before removing from the pan.

Carrot Cake Energy Bites

Ingredients

- 1 cup rolled oats
- 1/2 cup shredded carrots
- 1/4 cup coconut flour
- 1/4 cup almond butter
- 2 tablespoons honey
- 1/2 teaspoon cinnamon
- 1/4 teaspoon vanilla extract
- Pinch of salt

Instructions

1. In a bowl, mix together the oats, shredded carrots, coconut flour, cinnamon, and salt.
2. Add the almond butter, honey, and vanilla extract, stirring until well combined.
3. Roll the mixture into small balls, about 1 inch in diameter.
4. Place the bites on a tray and refrigerate for at least 30 minutes before serving.
5. Store in an airtight container in the fridge for up to a week.

Chocolate Banana Bread

Ingredients

- 2 ripe bananas, mashed
- 1/2 cup almond flour
- 1/4 cup coconut flour
- 1/4 cup cacao powder
- 2 large eggs
- 1/4 cup maple syrup
- 1/4 teaspoon baking soda
- 1/4 teaspoon salt
- 1/2 cup dark chocolate chips

Instructions

1. Preheat the oven to 350°F (175°C) and grease a loaf pan.
2. In a bowl, mix together the mashed bananas, almond flour, coconut flour, cacao powder, eggs, maple syrup, baking soda, and salt.
3. Stir in the chocolate chips.
4. Pour the batter into the prepared loaf pan and smooth the top.
5. Bake for 40-45 minutes, or until a toothpick inserted into the center comes out clean.
6. Let cool before slicing.

Blueberry Almond Crumble

Ingredients

- 2 cups fresh or frozen blueberries
- 1/4 cup almond flour
- 1/4 cup rolled oats
- 1/4 cup almond butter
- 2 tablespoons honey or maple syrup
- 1/4 teaspoon cinnamon
- Pinch of salt

Instructions

1. Preheat the oven to 350°F (175°C) and grease a baking dish.
2. In a bowl, toss the blueberries with cinnamon and a pinch of salt.
3. In another bowl, mix the almond flour, oats, almond butter, and honey to form a crumble topping.
4. Spread the blueberries evenly in the baking dish and top with the crumble mixture.
5. Bake for 25-30 minutes, or until the crumble is golden brown.
6. Let cool slightly before serving.

Lemon Coconut Bliss Balls

Ingredients

- 1 cup unsweetened shredded coconut
- 1/2 cup raw cashews
- 1/4 cup almond flour
- 2 tablespoons coconut oil, melted
- 1 tablespoon honey or maple syrup
- Zest of 1 lemon
- 1 tablespoon fresh lemon juice
- Pinch of salt

Instructions

1. In a food processor, combine the coconut, cashews, almond flour, lemon zest, and salt.
2. Add the coconut oil, honey, and lemon juice, then pulse until everything is well combined.
3. Roll the mixture into small balls, about 1 inch in diameter.
4. Store in the fridge for at least 30 minutes before serving.
5. Keep in an airtight container in the fridge for up to a week.

Sweet Potato Brownies

Ingredients

- 1 medium sweet potato, cooked and mashed
- 1/2 cup almond flour
- 1/4 cup cocoa powder
- 1/4 cup maple syrup
- 2 large eggs
- 1 teaspoon vanilla extract
- 1/2 teaspoon baking powder
- Pinch of salt
- 1/4 cup dark chocolate chips (optional)

Instructions

1. Preheat the oven to 350°F (175°C) and grease an 8x8-inch baking dish.
2. In a bowl, mix together the mashed sweet potato, almond flour, cocoa powder, maple syrup, eggs, vanilla, baking powder, and salt until smooth.
3. Fold in the chocolate chips, if using.
4. Pour the batter into the prepared dish and smooth the top.
5. Bake for 25-30 minutes, or until a toothpick comes out clean.
6. Let cool before cutting into squares.

Raw Vegan Cheesecake

Ingredients

- 1 1/2 cups raw cashews, soaked overnight
- 1/2 cup coconut oil, melted
- 1/4 cup maple syrup
- 1 tablespoon lemon juice
- 1 teaspoon vanilla extract
- 1/2 cup almond flour (for crust)
- 1/4 cup unsweetened shredded coconut (for crust)
- 2 tablespoons coconut oil (for crust)

Instructions

1. In a food processor, combine the almond flour, shredded coconut, and coconut oil for the crust. Pulse until the mixture sticks together.
2. Press the crust into the bottom of a springform pan and place it in the freezer to set.
3. For the cheesecake layer, blend the soaked cashews, coconut oil, maple syrup, lemon juice, and vanilla extract until smooth and creamy.
4. Pour the cheesecake layer over the crust and smooth the top.
5. Freeze for 4-6 hours, or until fully set.
6. Remove from the freezer and let sit at room temperature for 10 minutes before slicing.
7. Serve as is, or with fresh berries or fruit topping.

Dark Chocolate Almond Bark

Ingredients

- 1 cup dark chocolate chips
- 1/2 cup raw almonds, roughly chopped
- 1/4 teaspoon sea salt

Instructions

1. Melt the dark chocolate in a heatproof bowl over a pot of simmering water or in the microwave, stirring every 30 seconds.
2. Once melted, stir in the chopped almonds.
3. Line a baking sheet with parchment paper and pour the chocolate mixture onto the sheet, spreading it evenly.
4. Sprinkle with sea salt.
5. Refrigerate for 1-2 hours, or until the chocolate is fully set.
6. Break into pieces and store in an airtight container in the fridge.

Strawberry Chia Jam

Ingredients

- 2 cups fresh or frozen strawberries
- 2 tablespoons chia seeds
- 1-2 tablespoons honey or maple syrup (optional)
- 1 tablespoon lemon juice

Instructions

1. In a saucepan, cook the strawberries over medium heat until they soften and release their juices, about 5-10 minutes.
2. Mash the strawberries with a fork or potato masher until they reach your desired consistency.
3. Stir in the chia seeds, honey, and lemon juice, then cook for an additional 5 minutes, stirring frequently.
4. Remove from heat and let the jam cool to thicken.
5. Store in a jar in the fridge for up to 1-2 weeks.

Baked Peaches with Greek Yogurt

Ingredients

- 4 ripe peaches, halved and pitted
- 2 tablespoons honey
- 1 teaspoon cinnamon
- 1/2 cup Greek yogurt
- 1/4 cup granola (optional)

Instructions

1. Preheat the oven to 375°F (190°C) and line a baking sheet with parchment paper.
2. Place the peach halves on the baking sheet, cut-side up.
3. Drizzle with honey and sprinkle with cinnamon.
4. Bake for 20-25 minutes, or until tender and slightly caramelized.
5. Serve each peach half with a dollop of Greek yogurt and top with granola, if desired.

Oatmeal Raisin Cookies

Ingredients

- 1 cup rolled oats
- 1/2 cup almond flour
- 1/2 teaspoon cinnamon
- 1/4 teaspoon baking soda
- 1/4 teaspoon salt
- 1/4 cup honey or maple syrup
- 1/4 cup coconut oil, melted
- 1 large egg
- 1 teaspoon vanilla extract
- 1/2 cup raisins

Instructions

1. Preheat the oven to 350°F (175°C) and line a baking sheet with parchment paper.
2. In a bowl, combine the oats, almond flour, cinnamon, baking soda, and salt.
3. In another bowl, whisk together the honey, melted coconut oil, egg, and vanilla extract.
4. Add the wet ingredients to the dry ingredients and mix until combined.
5. Fold in the raisins.
6. Drop spoonfuls of the dough onto the prepared baking sheet, spacing them about 2 inches apart.
7. Bake for 10-12 minutes, or until golden brown.
8. Let cool on the sheet for a few minutes before transferring to a wire rack.

Chocolate Avocado Truffles

Ingredients

- 1 ripe avocado, peeled and pitted
- 1/2 cup dark chocolate chips
- 1 tablespoon honey or maple syrup
- 1 teaspoon vanilla extract
- Cocoa powder for rolling

Instructions

1. Melt the dark chocolate chips in a heatproof bowl over a pot of simmering water or in the microwave, stirring every 30 seconds.
2. In a blender or food processor, blend the avocado until smooth.
3. Add the melted chocolate, honey, and vanilla extract to the avocado and blend until fully combined.
4. Refrigerate the mixture for about 30 minutes to firm up.
5. Roll the mixture into small balls and then coat with cocoa powder.
6. Store in the fridge for up to a week.

Raw Energy Bars

Ingredients

- 1 cup almonds
- 1/2 cup dates, pitted
- 1/4 cup coconut flakes
- 1 tablespoon chia seeds
- 1 tablespoon honey or maple syrup
- 1 teaspoon vanilla extract

Instructions

1. In a food processor, combine the almonds, dates, coconut flakes, chia seeds, honey, and vanilla extract.
2. Pulse until the mixture is sticky and well combined.
3. Press the mixture into a lined baking dish or pan, spreading it evenly.
4. Refrigerate for 1-2 hours, or until firm.
5. Cut into bars and store in an airtight container in the fridge.

Date and Nut Energy Balls

Ingredients

- 1 cup pitted dates
- 1/2 cup almonds
- 1/4 cup walnuts
- 1 tablespoon chia seeds
- 1 tablespoon coconut oil
- 1/4 teaspoon cinnamon

Instructions

1. In a food processor, pulse the dates, almonds, walnuts, chia seeds, coconut oil, and cinnamon until finely chopped and combined.
2. Roll the mixture into small balls, about 1 inch in diameter.
3. Store in an airtight container in the fridge for up to a week.

Matcha Protein Balls

Ingredients

- 1/2 cup rolled oats
- 1/4 cup vanilla protein powder
- 2 tablespoons almond butter
- 1 tablespoon honey or maple syrup
- 1 tablespoon matcha powder
- 1/4 cup shredded coconut
- 1 tablespoon chia seeds
- 1-2 tablespoons water (if needed)

Instructions

1. In a bowl, combine all ingredients and mix until fully combined.
2. If the mixture is too dry, add a little water, 1 tablespoon at a time, until it sticks together.
3. Roll the mixture into small balls, about 1 inch in diameter.
4. Store in an airtight container in the fridge for up to a week.

Peach Sorbet

Ingredients

- 4 ripe peaches, peeled and sliced
- 1/2 cup honey or maple syrup
- 1/4 cup lemon juice
- 1 teaspoon vanilla extract

Instructions

1. Blend the peaches, honey, lemon juice, and vanilla extract in a blender until smooth.
2. Pour the mixture into a shallow container and freeze for at least 4 hours.
3. Once frozen, use a fork to scrape and fluff the mixture until it has a sorbet-like texture.
4. Serve immediately or store in an airtight container in the freezer.

Mocha Protein Ice Cream

Ingredients

- 2 cups unsweetened almond milk
- 1 scoop chocolate protein powder
- 1 tablespoon instant coffee or espresso powder
- 1 tablespoon cocoa powder
- 1/2 teaspoon vanilla extract
- 2-3 tablespoons sweetener (maple syrup, honey, or stevia)

Instructions

1. In a blender, combine almond milk, protein powder, coffee, cocoa powder, vanilla, and sweetener.
2. Blend until smooth and fully mixed.
3. Pour the mixture into an ice cream maker and follow the manufacturer's instructions.
4. Once churned, serve immediately or store in the freezer for later.

Zucchini Chocolate Cake

Ingredients

- 1 cup almond flour
- 1/2 cup cocoa powder
- 1/2 teaspoon baking soda
- 1/4 teaspoon salt
- 2 large eggs
- 1/2 cup grated zucchini (about 1 small zucchini)
- 1/4 cup honey or maple syrup
- 1/4 cup coconut oil, melted
- 1 teaspoon vanilla extract
- 1/4 cup dark chocolate chips (optional)

Instructions

1. Preheat the oven to 350°F (175°C) and grease a small baking pan.
2. In a bowl, mix together almond flour, cocoa powder, baking soda, and salt.
3. In another bowl, whisk the eggs, zucchini, honey, melted coconut oil, and vanilla extract.
4. Combine the wet and dry ingredients and mix until smooth.
5. Fold in chocolate chips, if desired.
6. Pour the batter into the prepared pan and bake for 20-25 minutes, or until a toothpick comes out clean.
7. Let cool before serving.

Almond Joy Protein Bars

Ingredients

- 1 1/2 cups rolled oats
- 1/2 cup chocolate protein powder
- 1/4 cup unsweetened almond butter
- 1/4 cup honey or maple syrup
- 1/4 cup shredded coconut
- 1/4 cup almonds, chopped
- 2 tablespoons dark chocolate chips (optional)

Instructions

1. In a bowl, combine oats, protein powder, almond butter, honey, shredded coconut, and chopped almonds.
2. Mix until fully combined.
3. Press the mixture into a lined 8x8-inch baking pan.
4. Freeze for at least 2 hours, then cut into bars.
5. Store in the fridge for up to a week.

Chocolate-Covered Almonds

Ingredients

- 1 cup raw almonds
- 1/2 cup dark chocolate chips
- 1 teaspoon coconut oil

Instructions

1. Preheat the oven to 350°F (175°C) and roast the almonds for 8-10 minutes until fragrant.
2. In a microwave-safe bowl, melt the chocolate chips and coconut oil together in 30-second intervals, stirring in between.
3. Once melted, dip each almond into the chocolate, ensuring it is fully coated.
4. Place the almonds on a parchment-lined baking sheet and refrigerate for at least 30 minutes to set.
5. Store in an airtight container in the fridge.

Sweet Potato Pie Smoothie

Ingredients

- 1/2 cup cooked sweet potato
- 1/2 banana
- 1/2 cup almond milk
- 1/4 teaspoon cinnamon
- 1/4 teaspoon nutmeg
- 1 teaspoon vanilla extract
- 1 tablespoon almond butter
- 1-2 teaspoons maple syrup (optional)

Instructions

1. Blend all ingredients together until smooth and creamy.
2. Taste and adjust sweetness with maple syrup if needed.
3. Serve chilled, optionally topping with a sprinkle of cinnamon.

Chia Coconut Bars

Ingredients

- 1 cup shredded coconut
- 1/4 cup chia seeds
- 1/4 cup almond butter
- 2 tablespoons honey or maple syrup
- 1/4 teaspoon vanilla extract
- Pinch of sea salt

Instructions

1. In a bowl, combine shredded coconut, chia seeds, almond butter, honey, vanilla extract, and sea salt.
2. Mix until fully combined and sticky.
3. Press the mixture into a lined 8x8-inch pan.
4. Refrigerate for 2-3 hours, then cut into bars.
5. Store in the fridge for up to a week.

Baked Coconut Donuts

Ingredients

- 1 cup almond flour
- 1/2 cup shredded coconut
- 1/4 cup honey or maple syrup
- 2 large eggs
- 1/4 cup coconut oil, melted
- 1/2 teaspoon vanilla extract
- 1/2 teaspoon baking powder
- 1/4 teaspoon salt

Instructions

1. Preheat the oven to 350°F (175°C) and grease a donut pan.
2. In a bowl, combine almond flour, shredded coconut, baking powder, and salt.
3. In another bowl, whisk the eggs, honey, melted coconut oil, and vanilla extract.
4. Combine the wet and dry ingredients until smooth.
5. Pour the batter into the donut pan and bake for 15-18 minutes.
6. Let cool before removing from the pan.

Vegan Chocolate Chip Cookies

Ingredients

- 1 cup almond flour
- 1/2 cup coconut flour
- 1/4 cup coconut oil, melted
- 1/4 cup maple syrup
- 1 teaspoon vanilla extract
- 1/2 teaspoon baking soda
- 1/4 teaspoon salt
- 1/2 cup dairy-free chocolate chips

Instructions

1. Preheat the oven to 350°F (175°C) and line a baking sheet with parchment paper.
2. In a bowl, mix the almond flour, coconut flour, baking soda, and salt.
3. Stir in the melted coconut oil, maple syrup, and vanilla extract until the dough comes together.
4. Fold in the chocolate chips.
5. Drop spoonfuls of dough onto the baking sheet and flatten slightly.
6. Bake for 10-12 minutes, or until golden around the edges.
7. Let cool before serving.

Coconut Lime Popsicles

Ingredients

- 1 cup coconut milk (full-fat or light)
- 1/2 cup fresh lime juice
- 2 tablespoons honey or maple syrup
- Zest of 1 lime
- 1/2 cup shredded coconut (optional)

Instructions

1. In a bowl, combine coconut milk, lime juice, honey (or maple syrup), and lime zest.
2. Stir until the mixture is well combined and the sweetener is dissolved.
3. Pour the mixture into popsicle molds.
4. If desired, sprinkle shredded coconut into the molds before adding the liquid.
5. Insert sticks and freeze for 4-6 hours or until completely frozen.
6. To release the popsicles, run warm water over the outside of the molds for a few seconds.

Healthy Fruit Tarts

Ingredients

- 1 1/2 cups almond flour
- 1/4 cup coconut flour
- 1/4 cup coconut oil, melted
- 2 tablespoons maple syrup
- 1/4 teaspoon vanilla extract
- 1 cup Greek yogurt or dairy-free yogurt
- Fresh mixed berries (strawberries, blueberries, raspberries, etc.)
- 1 tablespoon honey (optional)

Instructions

1. Preheat the oven to 350°F (175°C) and grease a tart pan.
2. In a bowl, combine almond flour, coconut flour, melted coconut oil, maple syrup, and vanilla extract.
3. Press the dough into the tart pan and bake for 10-12 minutes until golden brown.
4. Let the crust cool completely.
5. Once cooled, spread a layer of yogurt on top of the crust.
6. Arrange fresh berries on top of the yogurt, and drizzle with honey if desired.
7. Refrigerate for at least an hour before serving.

Raspberry Almond Muffins

Ingredients

- 1 1/2 cups almond flour
- 1/2 cup coconut flour
- 1 teaspoon baking powder
- 1/2 teaspoon baking soda
- 1/4 teaspoon salt
- 2 large eggs
- 1/4 cup maple syrup
- 1/4 cup almond milk
- 1/4 cup almond butter
- 1 teaspoon vanilla extract
- 1 cup fresh raspberries
- 1/4 cup sliced almonds

Instructions

1. Preheat the oven to 350°F (175°C) and line a muffin tin with paper liners.
2. In a large bowl, mix together the almond flour, coconut flour, baking powder, baking soda, and salt.
3. In another bowl, whisk the eggs, maple syrup, almond milk, almond butter, and vanilla extract.
4. Combine the wet and dry ingredients until smooth.
5. Gently fold in the raspberries and sliced almonds.
6. Divide the batter evenly among the muffin cups and bake for 18-20 minutes, or until a toothpick comes out clean.
7. Let cool before serving.

Chocolate Peanut Butter Energy Bites

Ingredients

- 1/2 cup rolled oats
- 1/4 cup almond butter
- 2 tablespoons cocoa powder
- 2 tablespoons honey or maple syrup
- 1/4 cup chocolate chips (optional)
- 1 tablespoon chia seeds
- 1/4 cup peanut butter

Instructions

1. In a large bowl, mix together all ingredients until well combined.
2. Roll the mixture into small balls, about 1 inch in diameter.
3. Refrigerate for at least 30 minutes before serving.
4. Store in an airtight container in the fridge for up to one week.

Coconut Yogurt Parfaits

Ingredients

- 1 1/2 cups coconut yogurt
- 1/4 cup granola
- 1/2 cup fresh berries (blueberries, strawberries, etc.)
- 1 tablespoon shredded coconut (optional)
- Honey or maple syrup (optional)

Instructions

1. In serving glasses, layer coconut yogurt, granola, and fresh berries.
2. Repeat the layers until the glasses are filled.
3. Top with shredded coconut and drizzle with honey or maple syrup if desired.
4. Serve immediately or refrigerate for up to 2 hours.

Dark Chocolate Coconut Energy Bites

Ingredients

- 1 cup rolled oats
- 1/4 cup unsweetened shredded coconut
- 1/4 cup dark chocolate chips
- 2 tablespoons almond butter
- 1 tablespoon honey or maple syrup
- 1 tablespoon chia seeds
- 1/2 teaspoon vanilla extract

Instructions

1. In a large bowl, mix together all the ingredients.
2. Roll the mixture into small balls, about 1 inch in diameter.
3. Place the balls on a baking sheet and refrigerate for at least 30 minutes to set.
4. Store in an airtight container in the fridge.

Pina Colada Protein Smoothie

Ingredients

- 1/2 cup frozen pineapple chunks
- 1/2 banana
- 1 scoop vanilla protein powder
- 1/4 cup coconut milk
- 1/4 cup unsweetened coconut yogurt
- 1/4 cup shredded coconut
- Ice cubes (optional)

Instructions

1. Blend all ingredients in a blender until smooth.
2. Add more coconut milk if the smoothie is too thick.
3. Serve chilled with extra coconut flakes for garnish.

Raspberry Sorbet

Ingredients

- 3 cups fresh raspberries
- 1/2 cup honey or maple syrup
- 1/2 cup water
- Juice of 1 lemon

Instructions

1. In a blender or food processor, blend raspberries, honey, water, and lemon juice until smooth.
2. Pour the mixture into a shallow dish and freeze for 3-4 hours, or until solid.
3. Once frozen, scrape the sorbet with a fork to create a fluffy, sorbet texture.
4. Serve immediately or store in an airtight container in the freezer.

Avocado Lime Cheesecake

Ingredients

- 1 1/2 cups almond flour
- 2 tablespoons coconut flour
- 1/4 cup coconut oil, melted
- 1/4 cup maple syrup
- 2 ripe avocados
- 1/2 cup coconut cream
- Juice of 2 limes
- 1 teaspoon vanilla extract
- 1/4 cup honey or maple syrup

Instructions

1. Preheat the oven to 350°F (175°C) and grease a small springform pan.
2. Mix almond flour, coconut flour, melted coconut oil, and maple syrup.
3. Press the mixture into the base of the pan and bake for 10-12 minutes.
4. In a blender, combine the avocados, coconut cream, lime juice, vanilla, and honey.
5. Blend until smooth, then pour the filling over the cooled crust.
6. Refrigerate for 4 hours or overnight until firm.
7. Serve chilled.

Coconut Pudding Cups

Ingredients

- 1 can (13.5 oz) full-fat coconut milk
- 2 tablespoons honey or maple syrup
- 1 tablespoon chia seeds
- 1 teaspoon vanilla extract
- 1/4 cup unsweetened shredded coconut

Instructions

1. In a small saucepan, heat coconut milk and honey over low heat, stirring until combined.
2. Remove from heat and stir in chia seeds and vanilla extract.
3. Let the mixture sit for 5 minutes to thicken.
4. Divide the pudding into small cups, top with shredded coconut, and refrigerate for at least 2 hours to set.

Apple Crisp with Oat Topping

Ingredients

- 4 apples, peeled and sliced
- 1 tablespoon lemon juice
- 1/2 teaspoon cinnamon
- 1/4 teaspoon nutmeg
- 1/2 cup rolled oats
- 1/4 cup almond flour
- 2 tablespoons coconut oil, melted
- 2 tablespoons maple syrup

Instructions

1. Preheat the oven to 350°F (175°C) and grease a baking dish.
2. Toss the sliced apples with lemon juice, cinnamon, and nutmeg, then place them in the dish.
3. In a separate bowl, combine oats, almond flour, melted coconut oil, and maple syrup.
4. Sprinkle the oat mixture over the apples.
5. Bake for 25-30 minutes, or until the apples are tender and the topping is golden brown.
6. Serve warm.